STUDENT
ESSENTIALS

Study Skills

Matt Potter

Student Essentials: Study Skills

This first edition published in 2011by Trotman Publishing, a division of Crimson Publishing Ltd., Westminster House, Kew Road, Richmond, Surrey TW9 2ND

© Trotman Publishing 2011

Author Matt Potter

Designed by Andy Prior

British Library Cataloguing in Publication Data
A catalogue record for this book is available from the British Library

ISBN 978 1 84455 417 1

Typeset by IDSUK (DataConnection) Ltd

Printed and bound in the UK by Ashford Colour Press, Gosport, Hants

Contents

Introduction: What are study skills?

Study skills are methods, habits and practices that can help you to make the most of your time at university and help you achieve the highest possible grades. Study skills are the range of approaches and techniques that successful students employ to find their way through the challenge of higher education studies, reducing stress while maximising success.

Many years of working with higher education students has shown that a grasp of key study skills equips students with an attitude and insight that allows them to engage with often complex ideas and arguments with greater confidence and efficiency.

Without an understanding of practical and useful approaches to studying, students often feel quickly swamped by their workload or disoriented by the expectations and pace of their course, so it's best to hit the ground running. This theoretically informed and carefully compiled collection of practical tips offers you a head start in preparing for your degree course and helping you manage the juggling act of higher education with greater clarity, precision and control.

This book is intended to be a practical guide for students of any discipline or at any stage of a university or college course. The aim of this book is to help you prepare for study by assessing who you are as a learner and by investigating ways of improving your time management and approach to critical thinking and research. It also offers useful advice on how to improve and develop a range of basic skills: from lecture and seminar comprehension to reading and researching strategically; from essay and report writing to giving effective presentations and revising for exams.

You will set yourself a number of short- and long-term goals over the duration of your course and reaching these targets requires advance preparation and a systematic approach. Ensuring that you can reflect a practical grasp of core ideas and concepts on your course doesn't happen by chance. Successful academic study requires meticulous thought and planning, and a familiarity with the essential study skills covered in this book.

It is assumed that students who read this book appreciate that there are no quick fixes or short cuts and that the guidance offered here will only bear fruit if accompanied by the dedication and perseverance required by any long-term endeavour. But the right approach and the practical advice offered in this book will serve you well as you navigate your way towards successful graduation.

Good luck!

PART 1

Preparing for study

Preparing for study means setting your compass in the right direction, and honing essential skills. It's about your approach to life as a university student. Orienting yourself in the right direction requires you to reassess who you are as a learner, and to focus on the attributes and skills you have and how best to adapt and use these skills for study. Beyond that, practical skills like organising your time and taking notes from lectures or reading are essential skills to master. All this culminates in the critical thinking approach to academic study; an approach that prepares you to complete assignments and engage with the ideas on your course analytically and critically.

1 Starting with yourself

As you embark on your university course, the prospect of tackling a heavy workload under time pressure while simultaneously reading and learning large volumes of new information can be more than a little daunting. Every new student experiences a mild sense of dread at some point and while there's no need to panic, there is a need to plan. There's a lot to manage and organise and the feeling that **there are just not enough hours in the day** is very common. So how can you get the most out of the time available? How can you effectively plan ahead and meet those looming deadlines? This chapter offers a number of different techniques to keep you ahead of the game and make being successful less stressful. And there's no better place to start than with yourself.

Learning styles: the journey begins with you

Getting the best from your time at university starts with the understanding that every student is different; not everyone learns and recalls information in the same way. There are different **types of learner**. Knowing which one you are (or which combination of styles or skills you have) can help you manage new information and assignments more efficiently.

There are three main types of learner – you might recognise yourself in the elements of one of the following types in particular, or you might recognise a combination. Whatever is true for you, if you feel clearer about how you like to learn things and then adapt your study habits accordingly, you will be able to study and learn more efficiently.

Type 1: The visual learner

If you're a visual learner you find the best way to memorise and make sense of new information is to 'see it'. You appreciate a lecture with clear visual aids (such as slides) that support the spoken information. You like graphical or numerical data in the form of graphs and tables and you value quiet study time.

If you are a visual learner the following good study habits suit your learning style.

- Drawing chronological timelines to trace events or describe scientific processes.
- Copying board notes during lectures or seminars.
- Asking the teacher to draw diagrams to clarify processes or ideas.
- Taking notes and making lists.
- Finding and watching relevant videos related to the topic.
- A system of colour coding words and research notes or using highlighters to circle words or underline key ideas.
- Using flashcards for revision.

Type 2: The kinaesthetic learner

Kinaesthetic learners are those who learn through experiencing or doing things. You're a practical type and may find it difficult to sit still for long periods, or you may prefer working in a science lab or conducting experiments. Often you will study with loud music or the television on or leave Facebook or Hotmail open on your computer browser. You might also be prone to taking frequent breaks when studying.

If you are a kinaesthetic learner the following good study habits suit your learning style.

- Studying in short blocks.
- Taking lab-based classes.
- Role playing or joining study groups.
- Taking field trips and visiting museums to enhance the learning experience.
- Using memory games or flashcards to memorise information.
- Turning off Facebook!

Type 3: The auditory learner

Auditory learners are those who learn best through hearing things. You may like to read aloud. You probably have no difficulty in sharing spoken opinions in class or seminars and you can follow spoken directions better than written instructions. You like presenting reports and giving detailed explanations orally. You're not afraid of being the centre of attention and as a result you contribute well in study groups. You're very talkative and can't keep quiet for long.

If you're an auditory learner the following good study habits suit your learning style.

- Using word association to remember facts.
- Recording lectures.
- Watching videos related to the topic.
- Repeating facts with your eyes closed.
- Actively participating in group discussions.

■ Keeping a recorded voice log of 'spoken notes' as well as writing them.

Once you are more familiar with the type(s) of learning style you have and the habits you could adopt to enhance your learning experience, you can begin to look ahead at how to plan your work, and that begins with setting goals.

Planning the road ahead: goals

'Start with the end in mind' is a good way to start your life as a higher education student. Visualising what your goals are is the first step towards reaching them. Picturing the finishing line and working towards it step by step is far easier than trying to fumble your way forward in the dark.

Ask yourself, 'What do I want to achieve in the long term?' You might answer: 'Achieve a first in my undergraduate degree.' This may be your long-term goal, which will be made up of any number of short-term goals, such as 'submit my assignment ahead of the deadline' or 'finish reading chapters 2–6 by next week'. Short-term goals should be targets you can realistically achieve and are directly relevant to the long-term goal. As you complete each one, you will have taken another step towards successfully accomplishing your long-term objective.

Don't work excessively hard, work SMART!

Action plans and targets need to be SMART. SMART is an acronym that stands for:

Specific: be as specific as you can be when setting your goals.

Measurable: try to quantify your goals. 'Read material' is not quantifiable, but 'read six articles' is. Charting your progress can help you stay motivated.

Achievable: be realistic. 'Complete all reading for first year in two weeks' is not only too general but also unrealistic.

Relevant: your task must be relevant to what you need to do.

Time-related: decide how much time you are going to allocate to your task every day or every week; even an hour or two a week or 20 minutes a day is helpful.

You can apply a SMART plan to each short-term goal to help you plan your time efficiently and work towards achieving your long-term goal. As there are likely to be a number of jobs that need work at the same time, SMART planning can help you divide time sensibly between various tasks.

Very soon a manageable and productive pattern of study will take gradual but definite shape. In short, you will be taking control.

Keep up the pace

We all know that sticking to plans over the long term can be tough. Different people are motivated by different things. To maintain your motivation, consider the following.

- **Work in concentrated bursts.** It's better to work in short specified periods than setting aside the whole day. Concentration is limited and you are likely to be more focused and efficient when you have a certain set period in which to work.

- **Reward yourself.** If you complete set tasks or reach set goals, allow yourself a treat! Check Facebook or call a friend. Have a short break or a chocolate bar. You'll feel you deserve these treats if you've worked for them.
- **Seek out support.** No one is an island. You can gain support and encouragement by enlisting the help of your study friends, tutors, library assistants, etc. The support is reciprocal and will motivate you not to let someone else down who has invested time in helping you. Your tutor or lecturer will always be happy to offer advice and guidance (within reason), so make the most of that offer.
- **Find what's interesting.** Discover what it is about your chosen subject that you really like; what it is that gets you excited. This aspect will ultimately link to other areas of your subject, giving you a broader appreciation of what you're learning. If you enjoy what you're studying, studying it should get easier!

All this planning is done principally to ensure that you are able to complete work within the set deadline; therefore, managing your approach to study is intrinsically combined with managing your time.

Time management: deadlines

Deadlines are part and parcel of university life. Different students treat deadlines in different ways. It's possible to divide them into three groups: the deadline-misser, the deadline-meeter and the deadline-beater.

- A **deadline-misser** is, of course, someone who lacks the organisational management necessary to submit assignments within the allotted time. They miss deadlines because their time hasn't been used efficiently.

- A **deadline-meeter** is someone who meets the deadline but only just! A deadline-meeter will get everything done (eventually) but often in a state of hurried panic. They spend a great deal of their time involved in crisis management – putting out fires and dealing with pressing problems. Many students argue that they work best under pressure, but the reality is that it only **seems** that way because it is only when the deadline is looming that they actually sit down and work.
- A **deadline-beater** is someone who is in control of their time. They tend to think preventively – which means that they make decisions and judgements that help them **avoid** crisis management by planning crisis out of their study life. They save time and energy by effectively structuring their time in order to prevent potential pitfalls later on.

Beating deadlines

To beat deadlines you need to prioritise. You must focus on productive ways to spend your time in order to reach set goals. How do you divide your time? How do you prioritise? Time is valuable and getting value out of it is essential.

Prioritise what's important before it becomes urgent

Stephen Covey, in his book *Seven Habits of Highly Effective People*, argues that prioritising activities is made easier when we are able to classify tasks more clearly. You should compare **urgency** (the pressing need to address an activity) with the **importance** of an activity (how vital or necessary it actually is).

- Activities that are **not important** and **not urgent** are activities that can be labelled time-wasting.

- Activities that are **not important** but are **urgent** are easy to get distracted by.
- Some activities are **important** but **not urgent**. Why wait until two weeks before your final exams to start revising? If you address important activities **before** they become urgent you are better placed to prevent a future problem from occurring.

Prioritise carefully and be a deadline-beater!

It's not all work, work, work!

You'll need to take a break! It's important to have time to unwind and chill out so that you can return to your studies refreshed and ready to get going again. Obviously there's a balance here. It can't be all fun, fun, fun either. But if you know what you need to do, when it needs to be done and how that work will be spread out realistically over time, you can factor in some 'you time' too. (And, incidentally, you'll enjoy that time so much more if you've done something to deserve it.)

Tips for top scores

■ Success in higher education has a lot to do with the right mental attitude and approach. You don't have to be a genius to succeed academically, but you do need to be organised and dedicated. Time spent planning and organising will never be time wasted.

■ Create a personal time survey. How do you currently spend your time? A personal time survey will help you to estimate how much time you currently spend on typical activities. Keep a record of how you spend your time for a week. You will be able to see where time is being wasted and will also get an idea of how much flexibility your timetable has, or will need.

✓ Dos	✗ Don'ts
✓ Clearly state your objectives. Set clear long- and short-term goals.	✗ Try to do everything at once.
✓ Follow SMART planning to ensure that plans are realistic and short-term goals are achievable.	✗ Put off until tomorrow what you can do today, i.e. procrastinate.
✓ Think preventively; prevent problems occurring before it's too late.	✗ Constantly assess the importance of tasks and ask yourself how they will contribute towards achieving your objectives.
✓ Spend some time investigating your own learning style to find ways of getting the most from lectures, seminars and self-study.	✗ Live in a world of crisis management; take control!
✓ Think positively! Positive thinking goes a long way.	✗ Struggle alone: ask for help.
	✗ Be a deadline-misser! Organisation and planning ahead make meeting deadlines more manageable.

2 Note taking and information organisation

Over the next months (and years) you will be generating a large amount of work. You will be reading a substantial number of articles and books and will need to record and keep information from these sources handy so that you can refer to them when completing assignments or revising for exams. It's worth spending time thinking about how best to organise these materials, and then implementing a system that helps you relate different aspects of your course. This way, you can find information quickly and efficiently and make sense of the ideas and discussions taking place.

Electronic filing systems

Setting up a filing system on your computer is reasonably straightforward. In the 'My Documents' folder of your operating system's file organiser, you can begin to set up a hierarchical structure of folders within folders. You can create, label or re-label folders as you see fit, and make links between them. These links should reflect the links between topics or subjects on your course.

The process of filing electronic sources of information is a good way to develop your understanding of the course components and keep track of where your knowledge or resources are low or lacking in depth.

Paper filing systems

Universities are still not paperless environments and even though computers have reduced the quantity of paper-based resources, not all sources of information that you gather will be in an electronic format. You will be taking lots of handwritten notes, will be given handouts and will make photocopies. Most of the time you can type up your lecture or reading notes and store them electronically; alternatively, you can scan almost anything and save it in your computer's filing system.

If you are still using a paper filing system you should buy a different folder for each subject. Colour code the files so that you can find what you're looking for quickly. You can also date and number your notes so that you know what lecture or seminar they came from.

QUICK TIP

Scanners are pretty cheap nowadays and a lot of printers come with built-in scanners – check your local high street electronic store to get a good price. Being able to scan documents to save them electronically saves a great deal of effort, storage space and retrieval time.

Note taking
Common problems

Taking notes at university is a fundamental and necessary skill. You can save time and effort if you master note taking, but taking useful notes can be tricky. There are three main issues that students face, especially when note taking in lectures.

1. It's difficult to stop or pause a lecturer to ask them to repeat main points until they're clear. Also, if the lecture contains a large volume of factual information, keeping up with the lecturer can be very difficult; you don't want to miss anything important.

2. Handwriting can be problematic. Writing quickly can produce illegible, poorly organised notes, which are less useful later for restructuring the information you've heard.

3. When you are taking notes, especially when reading, there is always the risk of plagiarism if you transcribe too closely from the original source (avoiding plagiarism is discussed later in this chapter and in more detail in Chapter 7).

Choosing the right note-taking style for the right job and developing your note-taking skills can help address these common problems.

Different note-taking styles

Below are some descriptions of a number of note-taking styles, for both lectures and written sources, and the benefits and drawbacks of each.

1. **Word for word:** verbatim, or copying every single word spoken or read. Useful for quotes but can make plagiarism more likely.

2. **Linear notes:** complete sentences and paragraphs – not verbatim, but notes written as full sentences. Good for lectures and reading – as long you remember to write the ideas in your own words.

3. **Spider diagrams:** branches of meaning and association linking various main ideas together like a spider's web; similar to

bubble charts and mind-maps. Good for lectures and reading as notes can be linked quickly and efficiently – but remember to write up these notes as soon as possible after the lecture. Also good for people with bad handwriting.

4. **Margin notes:** making notes or comments in the margin of articles or textbooks.

5. **Underlining or highlighting:** in textbooks or articles.

Remember, the style you use to take notes in a lecture is likely to be different from how you take notes from reading, so be flexible and choose the right style for the right job.

Abbreviate where poss.

A key technique that can help you keep up with fast-flowing information in lectures is to adopt a system of symbols and abbreviations when note taking. This saves time while making the job of note taking more manageable and easier to follow later.

Of course, only use symbols and abbreviations that will make sense to you later on. If you can't remember what your shortened note forms mean, nobody will!

Abbreviation means reducing the length of words. Think 'texting language' on your mobile: 'Gr8 2 c u 2day.' Of course academic abbreviations and symbols will be more complex and may be subject-specific. Mathematics students, for example, will have a vast array of symbols that are commonly used. Science students similarly will quickly learn various discipline-specific symbols.

However, students of any discipline can use some of the most common abbreviations and symbols:

e.g. (for example)	re (in reference to)	= (is equal to)
+ (and/in addition to)	etc. (and so on)	n.b. (note)
< (less than)	> (greater than)	→ (leading to)

Beyond this you can often shorten long words with no loss of clarity. This can be done according to a system that's personal to you. Remember, you will have to be able to make sense of your notes when you review them!

For example:

information = info
necessary = nec
organisation = org

Academic abbreviations such as the following can also be used in referencing.

- ***Ibid.*:** the same source as most recently mentioned is being referred to, meaning you don't have to repeat the author's surname.
- ***Et al.*:** used when a particular reference has more than three authors. Rather than trying to write down all the authors' surnames you can just write the first. Alphabetical order is usually used, and then *et al.* to indicate that there were other writers.
- ***Viz*:** in other words.

I've got so many notes I don't know what to do with them!

If you find you are recording too much information, either from lectures or from your reading, perhaps you're not being selective enough. Ask yourself the following questions to test the relevance of your reading.

- Am I clear on the assignment question? (See Chapter 6 for more on this.)
- How far does the information I've found or I'm reading go towards answering the question?
- Do I already have similar information?
- Will I actually use this information? If so, how and when?

Wider reading is good, but it's easy to become distracted and you can find that you go off on a reading tangent in which you waste valuable time taking notes on topics that are not directly related to the work you are trying to produce. Having said that, do allow some flexibility. It's entirely possible that you will come across information or ideas that you hadn't thought about, so as long as it's relevant include this unanticipated information in your notes.

I don't think I have enough notes!

Then again, perhaps the opposite is true and you feel you are not recording enough information. In which case it's possible either that you have temporarily lost focus or that you are possibly missing the key points. Again, go back to the assignment title and question the relevance or purposefulness of what you are doing.

Avoiding plagiarism

Plagiarism means presenting, intentionally or unintentionally, someone else's work as your own.

Plagiarism is treated very seriously by universities and can ultimately result in receiving a zero grade for your assignments or, in severe cases, deregistration from your course, so you have to take steps to avoid it.

It's always tempting to simply transcribe the words of the author from papers or academic texts as it's often difficult to say it any better than they have. Although it is better to attempt to summarise their views or arguments, it is also possible to quote directly from original sources using quotation marks to indicate this, for example:

> *'Students who plagiarise often do so accidentally'*
> *(Bloggs, 2009).*

Or even as a partial quotation, for example:

> *Tutors often report that students who plagiarise 'often do so without intention and are surprised when accused'*
> *(Bloggs, 2009), but this doesn't mean that it's acceptable.*

However, partial quotation is typically used for short quotations and less often for longer sections of text. In those cases you will need to practise the skills of summarising and paraphrasing.

- **Summarising** is the skill of capturing the main idea of a text or article quickly and briefly in a few words.
- **Paraphrasing** is different in that you are not necessarily making the text shorter but rather repeating the main idea in your own words.

In either instance you will need to record the source. This means noting the author's name, the date of publication, title of the article or book, the publisher and place of publication. See Chapter 7 for more details on recording references.

Notes from virtual learning environments (VLEs)

In addition to lectures and source reading, you will also be able to find information through the online learning resources offered by your university library and department. There is a variety of online websites, intranets and VLEs, so you need to ensure you have a system in place to help you take useful notes and file these notes correctly.

- Bookmark useful pages. These bookmarked pages can be labelled and stored as a record of research conducted.
- Work out a timetable for regularly visiting VLEs such as Blackboard. Your university is likely to have a VLE site for each department or even each module, where tutors will regularly post articles, important notices, lecture information and seminar topics. There will probably be discussion forums set up so that you can share ideas or concerns with fellow students or with your tutor.
- Ask your tutor how, where and when you can expect to find resources related to your course posted online.

Tips for top scores

- One immediate way to help solve the problem of note taking in lectures is to record the lecturer on a Dictaphone or your mobile. This doesn't mean you don't have to take notes, but it does mean that you can alleviate some of the pressure by knowing you can go back later and listen again to check your notes for accuracy.

■ As soon as you can, familiarise yourself with your department's VLE so you can get the most from online resources. Blackboard, for instance, will act as a constant source of reference and updates. You can also make use of online discussion forums, which are often available through your department's VLE; this can be an excellent way to keep informed and share ideas or concerns.

■ When taking notes, the principal task is to record the data, opinions and information from the reading material or lecture. However, you should try to assimilate the information as well as simply recording it. Put question marks next to ideas that clash or that you're not clear on. Recording these connections can help inform the direction of later research or reading.

✓ Dos	✗ Don'ts
✓ Set up a clear filing system – one that you can easily add to and retrieve from.	✗ Let the amount of notes or electronic documents you are gathering get out of control.
✓ Work out a style of taking notes that suits you.	✗ Transcribe notes directly from sources – try to paraphrase or summarise the main ideas in your own words. This will help you avoid plagiarism.
✓ Write up notes after a lecture so that the information is clear and recognisable later.	✗ Read everything you find – be selective. Ask yourself whether the source is relevant to make sure you don't waste time reading sources that won't ultimately help you complete your assignments.
✓ Alternate note-taking styles depending on what task you're engaged in, i.e. notes from reading, notes from lectures, margin notes in textbooks or articles, or mind-maps for brainstorming or lectures.	

3 Using knowledge to think critically

During pre-university study, demonstrating knowledge is often a case of collecting information from authoritative or expert sources, memorising that information and then repeating what you can remember in exam or coursework conditions. At university, though, there is an expectation that students will adopt a different approach and learn how to **think and analyse critically**. To do this you will have to read a lot of new information. You can't be expected to memorise it all! The happy fact is that you're not really expected to; in reality what you do need to do is **read critically**. This means developing your ability to extract key points from the texts which are relevant to your work and then analyse how reliable, valid or applicable the ideas actually are in the context of your discussion or research. This evaluation of sources is the basis of a critical thinking approach.

Kinds of knowledge

A first step towards reading and thinking critically is to consider different **ways of knowing** and different **kinds of knowledge**. Viewing information in terms of the **kind** of knowledge it represents will allow you to start analysing what you read with a critical distinction between what you **know** you know and what you can **support** you know through clear explanation, use of evidence and the help of data and statistics.

Let's consider two general types of knowledge as a starting point; **tacit** and **explicit** knowledge. Knowing the difference can help you to distinguish between **fact** and **opinion** and between **reliable** and potentially **unreliable** or **biased** information – all essential in a genuinely critical approach.

Tacit knowledge

How do you know how to speak English? If you use English as a second language, you may be able to explain more clearly how you acquired the language, but if English is your first language, explaining how you 'know' English will be far more difficult.

How you 'know' your native language is a form of tacit knowledge.

Key features
Tacit knowledge is difficult to pass on to someone else or to explain formally and systematically. Subjective insights, or having a 'sense' of something characterise this type of knowledge. Essentially, tacit knowledge is largely experiential; personal experience in the form of ideals, values or emotions.

Explicit knowledge

Teachers of English have explicit methods for explaining aspects of English language learning. They take something that is for most of us a tacit understanding and through study and years of research make it explicit. For example, there are aspects of the language, such as grammar, punctuation, sentence structure and syntax, which an English teacher can explain in detail, but which for native English speakers is automatic.

Key features
Explicit knowledge is made up of the things that an individual knows and can easily write down and explain. Universally agreed principles, statistical data and numerical data are all common forms of explicit knowledge, often gained through observation, reading or group discussion.

It is important to understand that there are different types of knowledge out there. Knowledge comprises different opinions and is supported by different kinds of research and data. How you analyse the reliability, credibility and validity of the information you gather on your course plays a large part in how well you are able to construct answers to questions and how deeply you are able to delve into any given subject. This investigation into and questioning of knowledge is the basis of a vital critical thinking approach.

The critical thinking approach

The critical thinking approach is a step-by-step process. Critical thinking is the process by which concepts, facts and ideas are analysed, internalised and comprehended. The steps that comprise a critical thinking approach are: knowledge, comprehension, application, analysis, synthesis and evaluation.

Step 1: Knowledge

Knowledge refers to the ability to memorise, recall and repeat information. You shouldn't worry about analysing a subject immediately after reading or studying it; instead, focus on understanding key terms and identifying main concepts. Questions at this stage might include the following.

- What happened after . . .?
- Who was it that . . .?
- Name the . . .
- Find the meaning of . . .
- What is . . .?
- Which is true or false . . .?

Step 2: Comprehension

Interpret, rephrase, explain

Here you already have the knowledge. What you need to do now is demonstrate an understanding of the material. Ideas are transformed and developed into the beginning stages of analysis. Students should be able to summarise, demonstrate and interpret the material, but since ideas are still in the development stage, we have yet to reach a stage of **full** analysis. Comprehending studied materials indicates that its main principles have been identified and are familiar to the student. At this stage questions might include the following.

- Write in your own words . . .
- Write a brief outline . . .
- What was the main idea . . .?
- Who was the key character . . .?
- Distinguish between . . . and . . .
- What differences exist between . . . and . . .?
- Provide a definition for . . .

Step 3: Application

Once you are comfortable that you fully comprehend the material's basic facts, you can begin to address problems or questions raised by the material. This step only requires a basic application of the material to a particular issue. An example of this could be applying newly learned legal principles to specific case studies. Questions at this stage might begin with these.

- Group by characteristics such as . . .
- What factors would you change if . . .?
- Apply the method used to some experience of your own.
- From the information given, can you develop a set of instructions about . . .?

Step 4: Analysis

Following your initial, basic application of your material, you can begin to break the material into parts and analyse those parts independently. This will include categorising, classifying, relating or distinguishing the individual parts. A thorough analysis usually requires establishing support for a belief, interpretation or conclusion. Typically, questions which ask you to compare and contrast, to explain **why** or to examine an argument are asking for analysis. Here are some questions that might be asked at this stage.

- How was this similar to . . .?
- What was the underlying theme of . . .?
- What do you see as other possible outcomes?
- Why did . . . changes occur?
- What are some of the problems of . . .?
- Distinguish between . . . and . . .

Step 5: Synthesis

After you have thoroughly analysed the material in question and have practised applying new ideas to scenarios or issues, you will need to focus on restructuring the material you have analysed. This restructuring step considers how different aspects of the material could be combined and what the potential result of the combination might be. Questions often ask for a creative response in which you piece together the information you have read from a variety of sources to discuss a particular theory or idea. At this stage, questions might include the following.

- Develop a means of . . .
- Propose a possible solution to . . .
- What would happen if . . .?
- In how many ways can you . . .?
- Create new and unusual uses for . . .
- Develop a proposal which would . . .

Step 6: Evaluation

Criticise, defend, evaluate
In this final stage of the critical thinking process students evaluate the material's concepts, ideas or reliability. This evaluation, however, is not subjective, but instead relies on an established set of criteria for the field. An example of a set of criteria is a particular methodology used during experimentation. Evaluation in terms of the concept's reliability or validity is conducted here to identify weaknesses. When answering these types of question, you need to do more than summarise the opinions or viewpoints of others; you need to draw conclusions. Of course, you'll need the support of others' ideas to back up your conclusion, but the evaluation step should attempt to offer an original insight wherever possible. Here are some questions for this stage.

- Is there a better solution to . . .?
- Judge the value of . . .
- Defend your position on . . .
- What changes to . . . would you recommend?
- How effective are . . .?

Don't believe everything you read: contesting knowledge

Most knowledge is contestable. It may well be supported by a clear, logical line of thinking, but that doesn't mean that you have to agree with it. If you can find reasonable grounds to disagree and can support your position with arguments, examples, details and facts, you will have demonstrated an appreciation of the different kinds of knowledge that are out there and how they relate to each other and to your research; doing this well will get you extra marks!

A lot of what you read can be interpreted either as fact or as the writer's own personal belief. Recognising the difference is vital.

Let's consider the example below and try to decide whether the statements constitute a fact or an opinion and also who the opinion belongs to:

> **"** *In 2007 the UN published a strategy for environmental protection in Latin America. Bernard Jones has argued that the UN strategy was insufficiently funded. The consequences highlighted the magnitude of this failure.* **"**

We can see here that a fact is being stated. The UN has indeed published a strategy plan. This is a **fact**. Jones (an authority figure in the field) holds the **opinion** that the strategy was *insufficiently funded*. The writer then adds their own opinion; *the consequences highlighted the magnitude of this failure.*

It's worth noting that simply because the expert and the writer happen to agree doesn't mean that NATO's strategy *was* in fact poorly designed and carelessly implemented.

You shouldn't assume that this analysis has become a fact because agreement exists. Critical analysis, even when defending a particular position held by the writer, should still consider alternative viewpoints. A balanced view is objective and objectivity strengthens any logical argument.

Tips for top scores

■ You will benefit from having a system you can use to break down questions in order to highlight the problem itself and to understand the examiner's instructions as to what you are required to say or analyse about that problem.

■ Early on you need to get to grips with the fundamental arguments presented on your course. The ability to analyse questions more deeply will prove difficult without the basic knowledge.

■ Incorporating the six steps of critical thinking into your study process offers you a systematic approach to addressing problems and assignments on your course. It takes time to put all of these ideas into sound practice, but if you embrace the critical thinking approach you'll find it's easier to get to the heart of the matter and engage more fully with the topics being considered.

✓ Dos	✗ Don'ts
✓ Think critically.	✗ Take short cuts with your assignments – break down the question and instructions embedded in the question to give yourself the best chance of providing the kind of answer the examiner is looking for.
✓ Evaluate sources for reliability or bias – this kind of assessment of arguments presented by writers in your field can be the difference between average grades and excellent ones.	✗ Underestimate the importance of a questioning mind and approach to your studies.
✓ Adopt a systematic approach to understanding and analysing questions or problems on your course.	✗ Take arguments presented by writers in your field for granted – question their arguments and methodologies to demonstrate a deeper comprehension of the ideas being discussed on your course.

PART 2

Improving basic skills (1)

A great deal of the information, ideas and discussions you will encounter during your course will take place in lectures and seminars. It is vital that you are able to get the most from lectures and are able to contribute well in seminars, whether this means leading a group discussion or giving a presentation. Ultimately, the ideas discussed in these sessions will make up a significant part of your written assignments, so it's crucial to understand the basics of how to organise and structure a written essay and report.

4 Lecture comprehension

Lectures are an integral part of university life. Most courses include at least weekly lectures which usually focus on a specific topic that is part of your course or module. Lectures will be one of your best opportunities to identify key issues and pick up tips for further research, so you need to be sure that you can follow what is going on and get the most out of your lectures.

What to expect from lectures

Lectures are different from classes in a number of ways.

- They take place in lecture theatres, often holding upwards of a hundred students, with the lecturer at the front delivering the content (speaking) while the students listen and take notes.
- A large amount of key information is delivered by the lecturer and students normally have the opportunity to ask questions at the end.
- Generally, lectures provide an overview of the topic areas you will be asked to cover. However, lectures can also clarify complex ideas – lecturers sometimes view lectures as an opportunity to explain difficult ideas or topics to students in an accessible way.
- Lectures raise awareness of key topics and ideas to encourage students to read and do further research, and also to help direct that research.

It is essential that you attend lectures because so much of what you are expected to focus on is presented in them.

Preparing for lectures in advance

You will increase your chances of understanding what you hear in lectures if you consider the topic before you attend. Many lecturers circulate pre-lecture reading tasks to students before each lecture. This doesn't mean that you have to know everything about a particular topic prior to attending the lecture, but if you have a rough idea of the general topic and possibly an understanding of some key terms or theories associated with the topic, you'll be better placed to make sense of the information you receive.

If you attend a lecture with no information or expectations of what's to come it will take you longer to get to grips with the lecture's main purpose. For example, imagine the following responses to the question, 'What's today's lecture about?' Which of these responses suggests a student who is best prepared for what will follow?

- 'I have no idea.'
- 'Something to do with history.'
- 'Something to do with the history of the Ottoman Empire.'
- 'It's about the Ottoman Empire around the end of the 18th century.'
- 'It's about the decline of the Ottoman Empire between 1828 and 1908.'
- 'It's about the decline of the Ottoman Empire between 1828 and 1908 and the socioeconomics of the Reformation era.'
- 'It's about the decline of the Ottoman Empire between 1828 and 1908 and the socioeconomics of the Reformation era: it's part of our Reformation history module.'

The student who gave the last response might in fact know little more about the actual topic than the student who gave the first response, but at least their mind is already focused on the specific topic area. They have already contextualised the purpose of the lecture in terms of the overall objectives of the module. In short, they're ready to go!

Ask yourself the following questions about each lecture before you attend.

- Where is the lecture?
- What time is the lecture?
- How long will it last?
- Who is giving the lecture?
- What is the title of the lecture? What is it about?
- What module on my course is it related to?
- What assignment questions relate to this topic area?
- What do I already know about this topic? (Brainstorm with friends what you already know.)
- What should I read before the lecture? (Ask your tutor for pre-lecture reading tasks.)
- Do I have any immediate questions regarding the topic – what would I like to know or find out?

Purposes of a lecture

Remember that lectures may have different purposes. They can be:

- **argumentative:** containing a thesis which the lecture supports with balanced objective argument
- **descriptive or explanatory:** a detailed description of a person, event, book, poem, article, phenomenon or principle explained with examples and expert opinion.

Keep these types of lecture in mind when reviewing the title of your lecture to help you prepare for the type of information you will be likely to hear.

Keeping up with the lecture

The lecturer is likely to refer to visual aids such as PowerPoint slides or handouts distributed at the beginning of the lecture or in the seminar prior to the lecture. Take time to look up from your notes occasionally as a lot of non-verbal information, signals or clues that aid comprehension, will be communicated by the lecturer's gestures and movements.

The slides will bullet-point the topics being discussed and will present the main ideas that you will be seeking to capture. Make sure to use these as a guide for listing sub-topics or useful headings in your notes.

Visual aids used by the lecturer will often be posted on the department's VLE after the lecture. Be sure to check whether the materials will indeed be posted online and familiarise yourself with how to find and download these important resources. You can then compare the original slides with the notes you made. You may find that you have missed some key information, recorded facts incorrectly or misunderstood the main point(s). Checking your notes against the original slides will also help you monitor how successfully you are managing to take complete notes during lectures. If you find a high degree of discrepancy between the notes you have produced and the original slides, you may need to re-evaluate your note-taking technique (see Chapter 2).

The language of lectures: direction cues

Following language cues from the lecturer can help you keep track of the direction the lecture is going in. The lecturer may be moving to a new point, adding examples, referring to experts or telling you what he or she thinks. Whatever the moves are, being familiar with the kind of language your lecturer might use will help you keep up. Here are some examples of the typical direction cues you might hear in lectures.

What the lecturer says (cue)	What the lecturer means
Now let's turn our attention to . . . Let's look at . . . Moving on . . . Now . . .	I'm introducing a new topic
According to X . . . X suggests/believes/reports/ proposes/states, etc. X agrees X disagrees X sees things differently	This is what writers or experts think
It's important to notice here . . . In my opinion . . . Let me say/add/clarify/explain But is this true/accurate/ relevant?	This is my opinion
For example/For instance . . . To demonstrate this . . . To illustrate this point more clearly . . . For instance . . . What this means is . . . In other words . . .	This is an example, explanation or clarification

Incidentally . . . By the way . . . . . . but I digress . . .	This is interesting but not vital or necessary
To sum up / To summarise . . . Let's go over the main points again . . . To conclude . . .	This is a summary of the main points

Asking questions in lectures

Although the main skill being tested during lectures is listening, some lecturers offer the opportunity to ask questions at the end (others invite questions as they go along). Don't be shy. If something's bothering you or you feel you've missed the point a little, seeking clarification from your lecturer is not a waste of anyone's time.

QUICK TIP

It can be almost guaranteed that if you're not clear on a particular point, a number of other students in the lecture will be feeling the same but will be too shy to ask. You'll be doing yourself and others a favour if you speak up.

Try to keep the questions as brief and uncomplicated as possible, especially if you are using English as a second language. The more direct your question, the more direct you can expect the answer to be. If you find that you're still unclear, it may be a good idea to approach the lecturer immediately after the lecture and ask your question again one to one. Alternatively, you could make an appointment with the lecturer to gain clarification, or even email them.

Extracting relevant and useful information from lectures

It's difficult to ensure that you will be able to extract every last detail from lectures, but good note-taking skills will certainly help (see Chapter 2 for more information on taking notes), and so will being prepared for the lecture.

A further technique to check comprehension of lectures is to arrange to go for a coffee with classmates immediately after the lecture to discuss what you've heard. Sharing ideas with peers is an extremely useful method of getting your mind straight and putting the information into a comprehensible order. Of course you don't have to agree with your friends' opinions, but those opinions are no less valuable or valid than your own. An alternative viewpoint can raise vital questions in your mind which may in turn inform aspects of your critical analysis of a given topic when writing your assignment.

Below are some questions you and your classmates could discuss to assess lecture content.

- Was the lecture interesting? Why or why not?
- What was the main point of the lecture (the thesis)?
- In principle, do you agree or disagree with that thesis?
- How did the lecturer support each side?
- What expert or authoritative voices did the lecturer make reference to?
- What is a good summary of the main topics or ideas?
- What was the main conclusion?
- How does this relate to other areas of the course?
- Was there a chronology of events (a timeline)?

You will be able to add more questions depending on the nature of the lecture and the assignments you are being asked to complete. Either way, peer discussion is a vital part of making sense of complex information and it's also a good way to meet people!

Tips for top scores

- Supplement your notes ASAP! The sooner you amend and rewrite your notes the better. The information will still be fresh in your mind, so use this vital window of opportunity to structure your notes so that they mean something useful to you when it comes to research or revision.

- Sit comfortably. Why not take something comfortable to sit on? Lecture chairs can be hard on the posterior and if you're uncomfortable it'll be harder to pay attention!

- **Listen.** It may sound like an obvious thing to say, but it can be tempting to doze off or let your attention wander in the middle of the lecture. Keep focused, ignore distractions and concentrate on taking notes that will be useful to your later.

✓ Dos	✗ Don'ts
✓ Attend your lectures. They are an important part of your course and they give you the opportunity to gather vital information.	✗ Skip lectures. None of the lectures on your course is irrelevant; all contain information vital to your studies.
✓ Make sure you have a clear idea of what the lecture will be about – including the location, time, date and lecturer.	✗ Kid yourself that just turning up is enough; be prepared to take notes, ask questions and engage with peers pre- and post-lecture.
✓ Brainstorm what you already know about a lecture before you attend, so you're 'in the zone' when you arrive.	✗ Ignore your VLE, as it is likely to contain useful information related to your lectures.
✓ Ask questions in lectures if you need confirmation or clarification of important issues raised by the lecturer.	✗ Suffer in silence! If you have any doubts, confusion or questions, it's better to ask than to be left in the dark.
✓ Spend time with friends after the lecture discussing your impression and understanding of the lecture content.	✗ Study alone all the time – speak with friends.

5 Taking part in seminars

Seminars are timetabled sessions in which your group, along with your tutor, meet to explore and examine the different ideas, themes or topics covered in your course. These can include topics from lectures or from course reading material related to the modules on your programme. Seminars offer the chance to exchange opinions or understanding with your colleagues with the guidance of your tutor.

Seminar formats

Seminars often have a more informal feel to them than lectures, and they are a vital and valuable part of your programme. The emphasis is on sharing ideas, opinions and concerns through discussion, debate and presentations. Some seminar sessions are given over to the tutor who will aim to expand on the content of lectures or even assignment topics.

You will often be asked to take an active, participatory role in seminars. This will most likely take the form of a group or individual presentation on a topic related to your lectures or possibly in response to reading given to the group by your tutor.

You may also be asked, as an extension of your presentation or as a separate activity, to lead a seminar discussion. Seminar-led discussions focus on a given topic or theme and the job of the seminar leader will be to guide the group through a discussion that explores aspects of the topic.

Whatever format the seminar takes, it is your participation, whether through listening or speaking (both equally useful contributions in their own way), that will determine how useful seminar sessions will be.

Preparation and participation

The key to participating successfully in a seminar is thorough preparation. Whether you're listening to a presentation or participating in a seminar-led discussion, you will need to make sure you're prepared. It may sound basic, but make sure you know what the topic of the seminar is and whether it is related to a particular article or text. You should **always** read any text related to a seminar. Without having some background information and accompanying notes that you can use easily during the session, you will be less able to participate fully and your understanding of the topic will suffer as a result.

You might bring notes written up from lectures or notes from reading you have done independently on the seminar topic.

If someone else is tasked with giving a presentation or leading a discussion, don't dismiss these sessions as a test of other people's abilities. Your ability to participate is also being tested.

It's good to engender an atmosphere of mutual support; remember, if you are supportive and engaged in other people's sessions, not only will you gain from the opportunity to examine your ideas and understanding of key issues, you are also likely to receive the same positive treatment when it's your turn.

Get the most out of your seminars

Seminars are not the time to be timid. You need to be actively involved to make sure you get the most out of these sessions. If you've got a point or you're not sure about what's being discussed, say so. All participation, as long as it's relevant and respectful, will be appreciated.

Giving an effective seminar presentation

Most people don't look forward to speaking in public, so if you feel nervous about the prospect you're certainly not alone. Typically you may find that your legs start to shake, you feel hot, your memory stops working so you can't remember key facts or what should come next; then you either can't force the words out or they come out so quickly that no one can follow you. There are a number of things you can do to help reduce these kinds of nerves, but by far the three most effective techniques you should consider to ensure things go smoothly are:

- thorough preparation
- rehearsal
- structure and organisation.

Thorough preparation

When you are given a title or thesis to work on as a presentation, whether it be in a group or individually, the need for thorough preparation cannot be underestimated.

Preparing for a group presentation

To prepare for a group presentation, you first need to agree on the position or angle your discussion will take. You will need to cover a number of topic areas, which will require individual and collective research.

This research should be sensibly broken down and distributed amongst the team, giving responsibility to each individual while still managing to co-ordinate a collective effort that works seamlessly as an argumentative whole.

Important as it is to be clear about what you're doing, it is equally important to know what other members of the group are doing. If one member fails to turn up on the day, for whatever reason, another team member may have to step into the breach – and that may be you! So be prepared.

Preparing for an individual presentation

Preparing for an individual presentation means you must take responsibility for every aspect of the presentation yourself. This is good in as much as it gives you greater control over the thesis and content. You are obviously responsible for the whole presentation, but that doesn't mean you can't rehearse with friends. In fact, you should actively seek out the opportunity to practise beforehand as it will ensure that your timing is accurate, make your delivery clearer and help calm your nerves.

Rehearsal

Once you have researched and addressed the set task with a critical eye and logical reasoning and have decided on a certain structure (amongst the group or on your own), the next step is to rehearse.

There is a clear distinction between those students who take time to run through their presentation and those who try to 'wing it'. The difference is stark and impossible to hide.

Being confident helps without a doubt, but people often find that the moment they stand in front of their tutor and their group, their confidence suddenly and inexplicably evaporates. The only genuine way of being sure that you will give an effective presentation is to put in the hard groundwork in the first place and to rehearse your presentation to iron out any kinks.

Structure and organisation

Whether preparing a group or individual presentation, you will be expected to have a firm grasp of the content of your presentation. What this means is that you cannot simply read your presentation word for word from a prepared script: this is called script dependency and could potentially cost you marks. It's better to refer quickly to flashcards with notes. Better still, using your visual aids

> **QUICK TIP**
>
> Timing can be difficult to get right, so practising your presentation in front of the mirror or, better still, your flatmates will help ensure that you stick to the time allocated to your presentation.

as an aide-memoire can prove very helpful. If you carefully bullet-point main topics and important ideas on your slides, this will jog your memory as you move through your own visual aids.

However, the best way of all to make sure your presentation flows smoothly and cohesively is to follow a strict and recognisable structure.

There are other possible structures available to you, but the classic oral presentation structure is perhaps the easiest and most logical. It follows an organisational pattern like this.

1. **Introduce yourself and your talk:** say 'Hello', 'Good morning' or 'Good afternoon' and state the general topic area of the presentation.

2. **Identify the purpose of your talk:** state what specifically you want to say, discuss or analyse with regard to the general topic area.

3. **Give your outline:** identify the main parts of your talk. Explain how you intend to argue your point. This will let the audience know what to expect, making it easier for them to follow you.

4. **State when you will take questions:** tell the audience whether they can interrupt or whether they should save questions until the end. Asking the audience to wait until the end is often a good idea as you can prevent yourself from being side-tracked.

5. **The body of the presentation:** present the information in the order you said you would. This order should be similar to the logical structure you would apply to a written essay.

6. **Introduce the conclusion:** use a simple phrase like, 'Well, that brings me to the end of my last topic and now I'd just like to quickly summarise the main points.' This is an example of **signal language** – language that helps guide and direct the listener. Now you have alerted the audience to the fact that your presentation is nearing a conclusion, those who might not have been paying close attention can sit up and get ready to note down the main points.

7. **Summarise the main points:** this ensures that the audience has understood them. You do not want to have to deal with questions in which you simply repeat information because the audience failed to follow you in the first place.

8. **Conclude the presentation:** wrap up proceedings strongly. Maybe end with a hope for the future. Make recommendations

for future research or acknowledge the limitations and weaknesses of your own work. Then thank everyone for attending and listening and invite questions.

Taking questions

Here are some tips for taking questions after a presentation.

- If you are asked something you are unsure of, try to avoid saying you don't know. Instead, ask the questioner what they think and bounce off their answer. Alternatively, admit that you don't have the full answer but will endeavour to find out and will get back to the person with a response as soon as possible.
- Ask for clarification if the question appears unclear (or if you need time to think).
- Be alert to questions that lack relevance to the topic or points being discussed. If you feel the question is irrelevant, you can suggest that perhaps it's a question for a different discussion or that you'd like to stay on track.
- Be robust and confident in your answers, but allow for criticism of your argument and accept it gracefully. You are expected to defend your position through the use of logical reasoning; but don't be defensive. If a point is fair in its criticism or point of view, accept it gracefully: agree that it is certainly a good point and worth considering.

Tips for successful presentations

Organisation

- Have a clear structure and a sense of timing. Rehearse your presentation to work out any kinks in timing and delivery.

■ Make sure you have a strong introduction and conclusion: these are the parts the audience will remember most clearly.

Delivery

■ Using pauses, stresses and changes in intonation for emphasis can keep the audience engaged and interested.

Body language

■ Maintain good eye contact with the audience to make them feel engaged and focused.
■ Try to project a positive, confident and relaxed manner.
■ Try to avoid distracting gestures or movements, such as blocking slides by walking in front of them, or moving around too much: this can break your audience's concentration.

Visual aids

■ Keep the information clear and simple – use bullet points. Visual aids should be attractive but not distractive.

Seminar-led discussions

You may be asked to lead a discussion within the group. The job of a seminar leader is to:

■ highlight a particular topic, discuss its main principles and then open the debate to the wider group for discussion
■ facilitate that discussion with carefully considered intervention and the ability to pit argumentative points of view against each other while remaining ultimately neutral.

It's a tricky balance to strike. You may choose to lead the discussion by asking relevant questions that you think would be beneficial, interesting and productive for the group to discuss. The point of the questions is to spark debate, but you want questions that will engage, not enrage! So think of points of controversy that will get the discussion started, but consider the wording of your questions or statements carefully – you don't want to offend anyone.

Open-ended vs. closed questions

When trying to generate discussion it's a good idea to think of questions which cannot be answered with a simple 'yes' or 'no'.

Closed questions can be answered too simply and hinder discussion – but with some restructuring you can ask the same question in a way that encourages a more thoughtful and detailed response.

For example, compare the following.

Closed questions
- Do you agree with the death penalty as a deterrent?
- Do you think the reintroduction of the death penalty is a good idea as a deterrent?

Open-ended questions
- What are the advantages and disadvantages of the death penalty?
- If the death penalty were reintroduced in the UK, what impact would this have on crime rates?

Guidelines

A good discussion leader must:

- have a good knowledge of the subject or topic being discussed
- stay one step ahead. Be prepared for the kinds of argument common in the field so that you can anticipate responses
- be flexible. Unanticipated but relevant responses should be welcomed and the leader should be prepared to allow discussion to flow
- guide but not dominate. Don't talk too much but be ready to guide the discussion back on to the right track when necessary
- maintain discussion focus. Similar to guidance, but remembering to frequently relate what's being said back to the original thesis or topic being discussed
- keep the energy levels up. Contemplative silence is fine, but silence can sometimes be like 'dead air' on the radio. If you sense that the discussion is falling flat, be prepared to jump in to reinvigorate it by asking other questions or introducing a new topic
- make sure that the discussion is objective. Summarise or rephrase the group's contributions and use them to challenge the opposing opinions held within the group. You are not there to create confrontation but to explore various and differing perspectives
- ensure a sense of accomplishment. Summarise the main ideas for and against the thesis or proposition and end by relating these points directly to the thesis or proposition
- end strongly. Thank the group for their contributions and perhaps reiterate the ground that's been covered.

Tips for top scores

■ You can clarify ideas in your own mind and use seminars as a testing ground for arguments that you can later use in your assignments. If you put forward an idea and argue for it, but find that it is dismissed easily by peers, you'll have saved yourself from having the same idea criticised in your submitted work, which could cost you marks!

■ For group presentations, divide presentation sections or topics fairly and avoid making one person responsible for all the key sections. You may even make two people responsible for each section so that you have a backup. Have regular meetings in the library or coffee shop to update each other on progress or problems. Stick together as a team and help each other out – after all, you could share the same grade at the end.

✓ Dos	✗ Don'ts
✓ Go to seminars prepared. As with lectures, arriving 'in the zone' means you can get straight down to business and maximise your seminar time.	✗ Be afraid to actively participate in seminars. If you rely on everyone else to do the talking you might lose the opportunity to develop your own ideas or have them challenged by your tutor and peers.
✓ Find out if there are any pre-seminar reading tasks or articles and familiarise yourself with these before you go.	✗ Rush when speaking in public. Take your time and try your best to relax. If you've done the groundwork and have rehearsed, you should have nothing to worry about.
✓ Be aware that when giving a presentation everyone in the room will want you to succeed. It's better for everyone if you do, and knowing this should give you confidence.	✗ Be scared to lead a seminar discussion – preparation is key. Don't forget to think of open-ended questions to help develop group discussion.
✓ Structure and organise your presentation so that it flows logically. A clear structure also helps you remember where you are when you're speaking.	
✓ Rehearse – iron out any problems so that on the day you're ready to go.	

6 Essay and report writing

The majority of your assignments will take the form of a written essay. There are many types of essay you may be asked to write and knowing the difference between these types will be key in ensuring that you submit work that:

1. provides an answer that the examiner is looking for

2. demonstrates an awareness of logical organisation and structure

3. is written in an appropriate academic style and register

4. demonstrates critical thinking.

Obviously, the core necessity to make sure you receive good grades for your written work is to know your stuff! A clear understanding of the question, good organisation and structure, a critical approach and an appropriate writing style are the skeleton around which you hang the meat of your knowledge – one doesn't work without the other. In this chapter we focus on the essential skeleton of your essay.

Direction words

The first step in answering a question is to consider the direction or instruction word(s) used in the essay question. For example, if the direction word is 'discuss', exactly what does this mean?

'Discuss' requires an answer that explains an item or concept, and then gives details about it with supportive information, examples, points for and against, and explanations for the facts put forward. It is important to give both sides of an argument and to come to a conclusion.

Below is a table of some common direction words you will encounter. Try to familiarise yourself with what each means and what it's asking you to do.

Define	Explore	Discuss	Consider
Account for	Explain	Contrast	Describe
Illustrate	Justify	Trace	Compare
Elucidate	State	Evaluate/ assess	Criticise
To what extent is X true?	Analyse	Prove/disprove	Summarise/ outline

Answer the question

All assignment questions are chosen carefully, worded carefully and are designed to test knowledge of a particular topic, usually from a specific perspective. To provide an answer that satisfies the examiner, we need to first understand the instructions embedded in the question.

To do this we can employ the **SPRE** technique. It's not necessarily a revolutionary idea, but it is popular because it is practical and applicable to most academic questions.

S = *Situation*
P = *Problem*
R = *Response*
E = *Evaluation*

We can use this model to break down or 'unpack' set questions. Let's take a sample question:

> **"** *Environmental problems will cause the biggest threat to international security in the next 50 years. Discuss.* **"**

First we identify the **situation**:

> *Environmental problems and their impact on international security.*

Second, we identify the **problem**:

> *Will environmental problems cause international security issues in the next 50 years?*

Third, we provide a **response**:

> *What environmental problems could cause international security issues? Why?* (provide evidence) *To what extent?* (provide evidence) *What kind of security issues?* (provide evidence) *Where? Geographical location* (provide evidence).

Finally we **evaluate** our response:

> *Is there enough evidence to suggest that these environmental problems will indeed create international security issues; and what are the weaknesses with these arguments? What can be done to prevent these problems, or is it too late? What will be the outcome should we fail to prevent these problems?*

The hardest part of writing an essay is getting started – but by using the SPRE model you can immediately break down the question into sub-questions and from this initial brainstorming start to build a basic plan for your answer. You now have a platform to work from.

Drawing up a plan using SPRE

Below is a first draft plan to the sample question used above (*'Environmental problems will cause the biggest threat to international security in the next 50 years. Discuss'*). This plan will need development – support, examples and details will need to be added or expanded on. But we can see that it's possible to move from a SPRE breakdown of the question to an outlined plan quite quickly.

Paragraph 1: Introduction (situation)
- Background: why are we discussing this? What have I discovered? Give key definitions where necessary so that the reader understands how you will be using key terms.
- Brief summary of the threats posed and whether governments need to take steps to avoid future problems. Where do you stand? (*thesis position*)
- How will this paper approach this question? (*outline*)

Paragraph 2: Problem
- An overview of the environmental problems and potential threats posed to international security to highlight more clearly the focus of your answer, before you move on to give explicit examples.

Paragraph 3
- Environmental problem 1: threat posed.
- What is it? Explain, define, give examples (including any references).
- Provide support for the idea that it's a threat.

Paragraph 4
- Environmental problem 2: threat posed.
- What is it? Explain, define, give examples (including any references).
- Provide support for the idea that it's a threat.

Paragraph 5
- Environmental problem 3: threat posed.
- What is it? Explain, define, give examples (including any references).
- Provide support for the idea that it's a threat.

Paragraph 6: Response
- What can governments do? What steps should be taken?
- What kind of international co-operation is needed?
- Who will take responsibility for the co-operation?
- Provide evidence and support.

Paragraph 7: Evaluation
- In response to the previous paragraph: how effective will the recommendations be?
- Is it too late to do anything?
- Will agreements need to become law in order for them to be enforced?
- Critically assess the arguments you have included from expert sources.

Paragraph 8: Conclusion
- Summarise key points.
- Reiterate thesis position.
- Offer recommendations.

Using the SPRE model and examining the direction words can help you draw up an initial plan of how you are going to answer the question. Once the information you want to include has been organised into a rough plan it's time to figure out an appropriate structure for your essay. You need to put together all the information and evidence coherently and logically.

Think logically: structure your writing!

Different questions use different direction words, so they require different responses.

Academic writers can make various structural and organisation choices, including:

- compare and contrast
- discursive: 'discuss' questions
- cause and effect: questions asking you to take a balanced look at a topic or angles related to a topic.

Two of the most basic (and the most common) organisational possibilities for answering questions are block organisation and point-by-point organisation.

Block organisation

Block organisation essentially does what the name implies. It divides two opposing aspects or arguments into two separate blocks.

- You can group ideas about Subject A in the first set of paragraphs or sections and the main points about Subject B in the second set of paragraphs or sections.
- You will follow a pattern represented by a 'vertical movement'.

This structure requires you to take each aspect from Subject A's perspective and say everything in one block (made up of as many paragraphs as necessary). Then you write a corresponding second block that details the similarities or differences between the same ideas, but for Subject B.

Figure 1

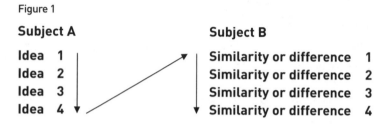

Some prefer this pattern because it is relatively simple, but one of the problems with block organisation is it can appear too basic. You may also find that because you're not directly challenging key points head on it tends to lend itself less well to a critical approach.

However, it is simple and easy to organise information in this way and as long as you provide enough supporting information from appropriate sources, there's no reason why you can't produce a well-supported, balanced answer to a set question using this organisational principle.

Point-by-point organisation

In contrast, point-by-point organisation allows the writer to treat the corresponding ideas on Subject A and Subject B as a pair and compare or contrast them one after the other or head to head.

You will follow a pattern represented by a 'horizontal' movement: you consider each idea head to head. This organisational approach repeatedly reminds the reader of the direct comparisons or contrasts between the subjects.

Figure 2

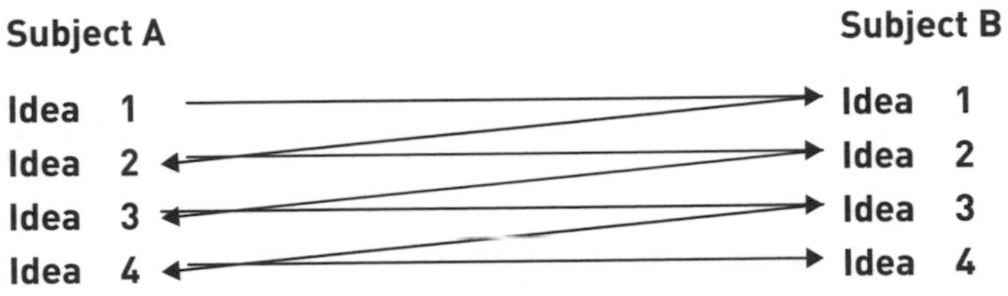

The problem with this organisational style is that it can become complicated to plan and write. There is a danger of repeating yourself in places and it takes careful planning to ensure that repetition is kept to a minimum. The advantage is that because it is relatively complex, a well-written point-by-point essay will impress the examiner and could gain your extra marks.

Lab reports

Science or engineering students are likely to be asked to write up experiments or lab work in the form of a lab report. As with any other form of academic writing, there are certain conventions that you are expected to follow. It is likely that your department will give you precise instructions as to how they expect a lab report to be written, and if you've already studied a science subject, you'll have a general idea of what to expect.

The typical layout of a lab report can look like this.

- **Abstract.** What are you investigating? What happened?
- **Introduction/background theory.** Why are you conducting this experiment? Include the hypothesis (your expectation of what you might find).
- **Experimental procedure.** How, exactly, did you conduct this experiment or investigation?
- **Results.** What happened? What did you discover? If you had a hypothesis, do your findings support that hypothesis or not?
- **Discussion.** Explain what you did and why you chose to do it that way. What did you discover or find and why did you discover or find what you did? What do your findings mean?
- **Conclusion.** A summary of what you did and what comes next.

Writing in the right tone and style (register)

When writing for academic purpose you have to make sure that you are communicating in an appropriate manner. Academic texts are written in a 'formal' tone. This tone and style of writing is often referred to as an 'academic register' or a 'formal register'. There are four broadly defined registers.

1. **The familiar register.** Characterised by the use of casual, conversational language, slang and features of spoken English. The rules of written grammar are often ignored. Think about texting on your mobile or writing a quick email to a close friend. This is obviously inappropriate.

2. **The informal register.** The tone is still conversational but less intimate than in the familiar register. There is still some slang and features of spoken English such as contractions (can't, won't, etc.), but the rules of grammar are generally adhered to. You might find this register in emails between colleagues who know each other fairly well. It's also commonly found in tabloid journalism – you wouldn't write an academic essay in the same way you would a news story in *The Sun*!

3. **The formal register.** This is the register in which most academic texts are written. It is not conversational and is characterised by formal vocabulary and perfectly observed rules of grammar. The tone is impersonal, formal, rational and objective. **This is the register you should use.**

4. **The overly formal register.** Characterised by the use of unnecessarily long and complex sentence structure using the most 'sophisticated' vocabulary the writer can find, often because the student has used the 'synonyms' checker on Word! This gives the impression of 'trying too hard'.

Ways to improve your register

You can do a number of things to improve the register of your writing.

Remove personal pronouns

Wherever possible avoid the use of 'I', 'We', 'You', etc. These words make your writing seem too personal and a little childish. If you do not mention yourself in your essay, it is usually assumed that the opinion expressed is your own. Therefore, it is often possible simply to omit the 'I' without any loss of clarity. Compare:

- '*In my dissertation I have outlined ...*' with '*This dissertation has outlined ...*'
- '*As I mentioned above ...*' with '*As mentioned above ...*'

Use the passive voice

You will improve the formality of your register if you use the passive voice so that no agent is mentioned. Compare:

- '*I decided to conduct the experiment ...*' with '*It was decided that the experiment should be conducted ...*'
- '*I designed the software program ...*' with '*The software program was designed ...*'
- '*I therefore argue that ...*' with '*It can be argued that ...*'

Remove all contractions

We use contractions in English to make speaking easier – *do not* is shortened to *don't*, for example – but in writing this purpose is redundant, and contractions make written English sound too conversational. Therefore you should use the full version of all words or phrases, for example:

can't = cannot
won't = will not
isn't = is not.

Choose formal vocabulary

This paragraph contains a lot of examples of conversational vocabulary.

'*The shareholders didn't **get** the dividends they expected. After **looking at** the figures they **found out** that some of the **adding up** had not been **done right**. Some of the key data had been mistakenly **thrown away.**'*

We can replace this kind of language with more formal synonyms.

> *'The shareholders did not* **receive** *the dividends they expected. After* **examining/assessing/analysing** *the figures they* **discovered** *that some of the* **calculations** *had not been* **carried out properly/correctly/accurately**. *Some of the key data had been mistakenly* **discarded.**'

Tips for top scores

- Support for arguments can come in many forms, most commonly quotations, previously conducted research or experiments and case studies. Facts can also be used to support your argument in the form of graphical or numerical data: tables, graphs and so on.

- Skim through scientific journals to get a good idea of what lab reports should look like and of the kind of language and writing style scientists use.

✓ Dos	✗ Don'ts
✓ Make sure you break down the question fully. This is your starting point and all that follows depends on how accurately you are able to understand the question and follow the instructions.	✗ Misinterpret the question.
✓ Be aware of the subtle differences between direction words. These differences can affect the direction of your work.	✗ Fit the question around what you know, fit what you know around the question.
✓ Remember that it's not just what you say that's important. It's also *how* you say it and the *order* you say it in. So the style and tone of your language (register) must be formal and appropriate for academic communication, while logical structure and organisation are essential in ordering information into a cohesive, well connected argument.	✗ Forget to proofread your work before handing it in. You will be able to eliminate mistakes in grammar, spelling and layout as well as inconsistencies in your argument.

PART 3

Improving basic skills (2)

To be successful during your studies you will need to add to the ideas and information gleaned from lectures and seminars. To write a genuinely critical essay you will need to conduct your own research and reading. This final part of the book considers techniques for researching and finding information. All of this knowledge will be tested in the form of written assignments and also in written exams. Preparing for your exams is an essential part of demonstrating what you've learned under pressure; following the useful advice discussed here can help you maximise your chances of achieving the best score. Ultimately, mastering all of these essential study skills will ensure that you are striking the right and most successful balance.

7 Researching and finding information

Greater learner autonomy (independence) is a feature of university life. The main purpose of research is to write essays and reports. The art of finding relevant information and then weaving it into your written work is essential to prove that you have a firm grasp of the subject and can discuss topics with a deeper understanding of the main issues.

On many courses you may be required to conduct your own research in the form of questionnaires and surveys, or through experiments that you design and implement. These are advanced research techniques. In this chapter we will focus on these more basic research techniques:

- preparing to research
- identifying sources
- using library-based and electronic sources
- recording references.

Preparing to research

As with any academic work, you should take the time to brainstorm ideas before you start your research proper. Review the SPRE model in Chapter 6 to remind yourself about breaking down the question to aid your brainstorming session.

> ❝ *Capital punishment should be reintroduced into the UK. Discuss.*❞

If this is your topic, the first thing to do is to ask yourself these questions.

- What does the question mean? Are there any words I need a clear definition of?
- What do I know about this topic already?
- What do I need to know?
- What are the arguments for and against the proposition (argument) presented in the question?

You can jot down your ideas in the form of a spider diagram or mind-map. To draw a mind-map, write the main idea in a circle in the centre of the page and then draw connecting branches with relevant ideas until a map of interconnecting ideas and questions links together.

Noting down your initial ideas is only the starting point – now you will have to find supporting information in response to the points you've worked out. Your research now has a direction for you to follow, but you should be prepared for your direction to change when you read more deeply into the subject.

Identifying sources

Now that you have identified the direction of your research you need to identify the sources you are going to use to conduct this research. First, let's consider two typical sources of information: books and journals.

Books

Higher education (HE) courses will often have set course books. Every student will be given, or will have to buy, these books. There might also be a recommended reading list of other books that are important for your course. These are the titles you should use to begin your research.

You can speed up your ability to pick out relevant sections in a book or article by developing your reading skills, such as skimming and scanning.

- **Skimming** is reading through a passage very quickly, gathering the gist (main idea) without concentrating on any specifics.
- **Scanning** is more intensive. Start with a mental list of key words or phrases that you are looking for; scan the passage until you spot key words; then read around them for specific information and comprehension.

Journal articles

Most academic subjects will have journals, specifically related to the subject, that are published annually, or even monthly. Often journals offer the 'cutting-edge' perspective of current researchers in the field. Researchers often establish their reputation through journal articles and you will soon begin to recognise their names as influential in your area.

However, it's worth remembering that there are a large number of journal articles out there: you need to be selective because there simply isn't time to read every article from beginning to end. In order to speed up the process, you can focus on specific articles or specific sections of articles to answer general questions of relevance to your research.

To help identify which articles are relevant to your topic you should look at the following.

The abstract
The abstract tells you:

- what the study is about
- what questions the writer was answering
- their general findings.

The abstract is a summary of the article and by reading it you will quickly be able to tell if the article is relevant to your purposes or not.

The literature review
A literature review is a list of what other writers in the field have said about a topic. It will help you judge the relevance and quality of the article. This is a good way to expand your reading. Go to the end of the article and check the reference section – this is a list of all the books and other resources the writer of the article referred to. You can then find the articles or books written by these other authors to find out more about what they said.

The discussion and conclusion
Scanning these sections will help you understand what the results mean (according to the author's interpretation) and how and where they might be applied and by whom.

The internet

Internet literacy is a key life skill. Being comfortable with knowing what kind of information is appropriate to you, where it can be found and how to search for it are essential academic skills. The internet has not yet rendered the library obsolete, but most students now turn to the internet as a first port of call for research.

The internet is an excellent research tool if you know how to use it. 'Googling' ideas is certainly one way to get started, but search engines can be instructed to tailor searches more specifically. You can conduct an advanced search on Google in which you limit your search to specific key words, while omitting other more general terms, to lead you to sites or articles that are directly relevant to your research.

However, while the internet can be a good friend it can also be a bad enemy. Some truly awful work is submitted by students who do quick searches on the internet and cobble together an assignment based on bits and bobs that have been copied and pasted from a variety of unidentified sources. The purpose of assignments is to demonstrate critical thinking, which means making reasoned choices about what information is relevant and reliable and then assessing the arguments put forward by authors in the light of your research question. Picking random examples from the internet does not demonstrate critical thinking.

Checking the reliability of sources

It's very important to be able to distinguish between the vast amount of 'good' information, which is reliable, unbiased, accurate and relevant, and 'bad' information, which is basically the opposite. Follow the checklist questions below to assess the reliability of sources of information.

1. How does it look (font, layout)? Is it academic, accredited by a reliable institution?

2. Is it on topic? Is it connected to and specific enough for your area of research?

3. Does it acknowledge both sides of the argument? Is it impartial? Is it balanced or serving a biased agenda?

4. If it presents raw data, how was the data gathered? How was information collated? Is the method of gathering data reliable?

5. Where does it come from? Is it from a university or professional body? Is it peer reviewed (reviewed by other experts in the field to ensure reliability)? Consider nationality – does the writer's background affect the focus of the research? This is concerned with the reputation and reliability of the author.

6. Is the research current, or is it outdated or made redundant by more advanced or relevant research?

Your eventual grade will be higher if you are selective about which sources you choose to include in your argument.

Using the library

Another essential source of information is the library. Each university will have a different system, so find out which system yours uses. The more familiar you become with your library set-up, the easier it will be to use the library to its full potential.

Part of your induction to a new course should consist of a library tour. The tour will show you the various features of your library, such as the study rooms and where various subject shelves are located. You should also be told how to borrow books and the difference between short loans (a few hours) and long loans (a week or more). Short loan books are often the most popular books that are in high demand, but there will probably be a booking system which you should familiarise yourself with.

Databases and catalogues

You should also be told about the library's databases and catalogues. Catalogues tell you everything that's in the library, while databases tell you everything that exists, some of which may not be available in your actual library. When you are looking for a particular title the library will check their catalogue first to see if they have the book available on site. If they find that they don't have it they can check the database to see where it can be obtained.

> **QUICK TIP**
> If you miss the library tour during your induction you should arrange an alternative tour with a member of the library staff.

Avoiding plagiarism

When making reference to a large number of different sources it is essential to keep track of whose ideas you are using. If you comment on, interpret or quote someone else's work you **must** make reference to the original author.

The importance of referencing

There are few undisputed facts. This means that knowledge can be contested or argued against. Often information is the basis of someone's research and as a result can be questioned. Most knowledge is based on theories/models/claims, which are **someone's work**.

Academic study (i.e. research) consists of evaluating existing ideas, seeing problems and gaps in knowledge and proposing something new or better. In this way, research can be seen as a kind of **conversation**.

Citing other people's work shows:

- how well focused you are on the issue: you have used relevant sources
- that there is evidence for your claims
- that there is justification for your arguments
- that you are engaging in the conversation
- that you are able to maintain a systematic, accurate record of your reading.

You should **always** provide a reference for the following.

- Quotations, paraphrases, summaries.
- Statements used as evidence which are not 'common knowledge', e.g.:
  - 'American cultural hegemony is destroying local traditions all over the world.' *This is someone's opinion and is not common knowledge.*
  - 'The process can be repeated to extend the single chain of polyethylene until the reaction is terminated.' *This is a specific scientific finding and not, therefore, common knowledge.*
- Distinctive or authoritative ideas, whether you agree with them or not.
- A summary of someone's ideas: a shorter version of what was originally said by the author.
- A paraphrase: rephrasing someone else's ideas in your own words.
- A direct quotation: repeating what someone has said word for word.
- Graphic information (e.g. figures, illustrations, tables).
- Numerical information (e.g. code, formulae).

You do **not** need to provide a reference for the following.

- Generally known facts, e.g. 'Facebook was launched by Mark Zuckerberg in February 2004.'
- Basic technologies, e.g. 'C++ is a statistically-typed, free-form, multi-paradigm, compiled, general-purpose program language.'
- Terminology, e.g. ' "Blog", short for "web log", is a personal diary or reflection, usually updated on a regular basis.'

Know how to cite

There are two internationally recognised systems for referencing: **Harvard** (name and date) and **Vancouver** (numeric). You should check with your department to make sure which referencing style you will be expected to use.

The Harvard system
The Harvard system (also referred to as APA style) is the system most commonly used across the disciplines. Whenever you refer to a document, include the author's surname and the year of publication in brackets, e.g.:

'In a recent article (Davis, 2005) it was suggested that . . .'

or you can include the author's name in your sentence:

'Davis (2005) discusses . . .'

If there are more than three authors, give the surname of the first followed by *et al.*:

'In an earlier study (Bloggs et al., 2003) . . .'

When citing a book you should include the surname, first name or initial, *Title* (Place of publication, Publisher, Year of publication) e.g.:

> Culley, W. *Business Ventures.* (New York: McGraw Hill, 1984).

The Vancouver system
The Vancouver system is used mainly in medical disciplines. Check with your department to see which they prefer you to use.

> Gray, H. *Gray's Anatomy*. Facsimile of 1901 edition (Philadelphia, PA: Running Press).

Referencing a website

To reference a website you should note the surname, initial, year of publication, title of article, indication that source was found online, place of publication, URL address, and the date you accessed the website on line:

> Burgess, T. (2005) *In-text Citations [on-line]*. London. Oxford Street College. Available from: http://www.Oxfordcollege.ac.uk/library/using/harvard_system.html [Accessed 17 June 2005].

It is not unusual for students to be unable to find all this information for web references. If you can't find the information required then it's acceptable to omit it. However, the URL is essential.

Citing a journal article

When citing a journal article you should list the surname, initial, year of publication, title of journal article, title of journal, volume, and page number(s):

Meloy, C. (1985), 'Outside Viewing' in *Watchers Digest,* Apr/May, 2–8.

Tips for top scores

- Compile your bibliography as you research and write: this will make the process of referencing much easier.

- It's important to maintain a web address filing system so that you can quickly find useful resources again. You can bookmark useful sources or copy and paste the URL into a separate folder for later reference. Keeping a system like this will also help you to minimise plagiarism.

- Take time to brainstorm in a study group. What do your friends think? What opinions or ideas do they have? You'll be surprised what new directions and inspirations come from having pre-research discussions with your classmates.

- Your academic department may have its own library home page, usually accessed via your subject's home page on your university library's home page. It is a good idea to bookmark this page on your browser as it will act as a portal to more advanced searches.

✓ Dos	✗ Don'ts
✓ Familiarise yourself with your campus library.	✗ Limit your search to only a few books or articles – where possible, conduct a wider search to get to the heart of the issue.
✓ Find out how to access databases and library catalogues.	✗ Forget to record references of everything you need, so as to avoid accusations of plagiarism later.
✓ Follow a clear checklist to assess the reliability of sources as you find them.	✗ Forget to make the most of the resources made available to you – the internet, VLEs in your department or university and the library.
✓ Ask your department what referencing system you should be using.	✗ Be afraid to ask for help with your searches – library assistants, tutors, lecturers and even peers can all have valuable ideas to help direct your research.

8 Revision and exams

No one likes taking exams. It would be strange if they did! But thorough revision and good preparation can remove some of the stress and anxiety associated with exam taking and help ensure that you perform to the best of your ability when it matters most.

Common exam myths

Exams are a source of stress and anxiety for almost everyone. However, it's useful to know that this anxiety is based on beliefs about exams which are not necessarily true. Let's start by dispelling a few commonly held beliefs.

1. **You can only be successful in exams if you have a great memory.** Not true. Exams often test your ability to develop and defend an argument. This has something to do with memory, of course, but what you are actually doing is developing ideas raised in the course. There is key information related to these ideas, but this information (names, dates, facts, theories) does not need to be remembered independently of other ideas; everything is connected and it is the strength of these connections that reduces the need for 'pure memory' alone.

2. **Exam questions are designed to intentionally 'catch you out'.** Exam questions are not written by sadists! The questions set in exams are meant to test you, but not unfairly. Exam questions are designed to offer you the opportunity to demonstrate your grasp of the course. It's a test of what you do know,

not necessarily what you don't. If there are any gaps in your knowledge, this may well be clear to the examiner, but it's how well you use the information you do have that's important.

3. **If I write down every name, fact, example, date and theory I can remember I'll get better grades.** Unfortunately not. You must fit what you know to the question, not fit the question around what you know. Review the information in this book to see how to quickly break questions down. You should include citations, examples and other kinds of information, but only where appropriate and relevant.

4. **If I fail, that's the end of my university career.** Most universities offer the opportunity to resit failed exams, but don't make this part of your plan! You might find it comforting to discover the rules concerning resits set out by your department in your university. Rules differ, but you will find that even final exams are often not limited to only one shot. Not only that, many people who fail at university go on to be enormously successful – Einstein and Freud to name just two!

5. **Last-minute 'cramming' is the best way to retain information before an important exam.** Exam revision should be well structured and can begin as early as possible. Waiting until the last minute is a risky strategy. Constructing information into a pattern that makes sense to you and incorporating the key aspects of the course takes time and is a systematic process. If you leave this process too late, you are placing yourself under even greater pressure than necessary. You often see students who are about to go into exams frantically reading books or notes: while there's nothing wrong with this – and it's true that key facts and examples read just before an exam stay fresher in the mind – if that last-minute rush is all you've done you could find yourself in trouble. Make sure you're thoroughly prepared.

Get your revision materials together

It is at this point that you'll appreciate keeping notes, photocopies, course notes and other relevant material well organised and filed. Set aside some time to decide what course material will be necessary or helpful for your revision. The process of organising your materials will bring into clearer focus the shape of the course itself. Divide information into topic areas covered on your course. You will be able to make the links between topics clearer and group relevant materials together. This isn't a simple process and it requires a lot of thought, but it is an excellent starting point.

Devise a revision timetable

Once you feel comfortable that you have put together all of the necessary material you can start making a revision timetable.

It's essential to spend time thinking about how best to organise your revision time. Drawing up a timetable will help you identify where in your weekly schedule you have sufficient time to dedicate to study. You will need to allocate the topics you need to revise to the slots you identify as being free.

You may be tempted to give more time to the areas of your course where you feel strongest, but resist this temptation; you should aim to devote equal time to each subject area.

It's a good idea to make a list of what needs to be covered for each module in order to determine how long needs to be spent on each section.

Try to avoid making your timetable too complicated. Keep it practical and workable. Don't make a timetable that you don't feel confident you can follow; but at the same time don't underestimate how much work will need to be done. Striking the right balance depends on the individual, but be aware that you need to have a strict, well-structured, day-to-day timetable that covers all areas and won't leave you exhausted.

Getting started with revision

It's not a great idea to see revision as a job that needs doing at some point in the future as the exams get ever closer. Saving up your revision as a single almighty task makes the process more daunting and ultimately less practical and constructive.

You should start by identifying which topics from your course are either the most important or the most likely to come up on exam papers. Don't worry too much about missing out some topics: you can't realistically (and are not expected to) remember absolutely everything. If you make a list of the main topics on the course and choose the ones you're going to revise you can then begin to organise your course material.

Summary notes

For each subject area write summary notes of the key ideas, arguments and details. This is an ideal opportunity to cut and paste extracts from electronic notes that you have compiled. Organise them by topic and add to them as new information comes up during your revision.

Sets of summary notes can be easily transported around with you and can be used for a quiet spot of memory revision on the bus, train or in the park.

Using past exam papers

You can also review past papers to get an idea of the type of questions typically asked. Your department will have an archive of past exam papers, and you can probably find these either through the library or your department's VLE.

You can use past exam papers in a number of different ways.

- To practise answering exam questions specifically related to your field and to look at the kinds of topic areas in your course that examiners have focused on in previous years.
- To get a sense of the kind of exam questions you can expect. You may spot trends and be able to identify favourite types of questions which, although the wording may have changed, have been asked before.
- You will be able to write model answers which you can ask your tutors to take a look at and give you feedback on.
- You will also be able to familiarise yourself with the layout and instructions that examiners use on exam papers, so that when you finally sit in the exam room and turn over the paper, it won't come as a huge shock – instead you can just get started! You should familiarise yourself with important details, for example:
  - How many questions are set?
  - How many sections is the exam paper divided into?
  - How many questions do you have to answer and how many from each section?
  - How long do you have in total?
  - How many marks does each question/section carry?

- You can practise writing under time pressure with past exam questions. Set yourself the same amount of time as stipulated on the paper and sit a mock exam.

Reviewing past papers can:

- build confidence
- help you become familiar with the layout of the exam paper
- help you identify commonly recurring themes
- focus your mind on key definitions, terminology or key words associated with your course
- help you sidestep tricky questions or answers by reducing the surprise these types of questions might give you if you came across them for the first time in the real exam.

Study together

Studying with friends is a good way to motivate yourself and to cover angles and perspectives that you might miss if you choose to study alone. It can help reduce anxiety if you diffuse the tension of exams by sharing your study experience with friends. Of course, you can't study in groups all the time as it won't be practical or possible in terms of availability.

Just before the exam

In the last couple of days before the exam date, concentrate on what you already know and have gathered together. The old adage, 'If you don't know it by now, you'll never know it' has some relevance here. Go through your summary notes and think about how this information might manifest itself in exam questions.

You'll be challenged to demonstrate a lot of knowledge and information in a very short time. Spend time visualising the answers or arguments you can construct in response to potential questions. This mental preparation puts

QUICK TIP

Set your alarm clock! If you don't live on campus, check that bus and train routes are running normally.

you in the pragmatic frame of mind you need for approaching a time-pressured situation where you need to be alert and sharp.

On the day

Make sure you're clear on the arrangements.

- Where is the exam taking place?
- What time will the exam start and finish?
- What are you allowed to bring with you? It's rare, but for some courses (law, for example) students are permitted to bring certain books or materials with them. Check the exam regulations to see what you're allowed.
- What equipment are you allowed? A pen? A pencil? Tipp-Ex? Can you take a calculator?

Getting the best results

Bear in mind the following points to help you get the best possible results from your exam.

1. Answer the set question. Breaking down the question and focusing on exactly what the examiner is asking you to do is essential. If you misunderstand the question, the chances of your supplying an appropriate, accurate answer is massively reduced.

2. Take time to see how many marks each question carries. If a question carries only one mark, it's likely that you only need to give a short answer or that a specific piece of information is needed. If a question carries two marks it's very possible that there are two parts to the answer. If five marks are available, the question probably requires a longer, more detailed answer. Looking at the marks attached to each question acts as a good benchmark of how much information is required.

3. Don't be scared of stating the obvious. Support answers with examples, facts, details, relevant names, quotes and definitions, but make sure these pieces of supporting information are relevant to the question.

4. Include diagrams or charts to support arguments or facts where appropriate.

5. Go into sufficient depth in your answer when necessary. Don't just skim the surface; demonstrate your knowledge with confidence.

6. Manage your time. How many questions are there to be answered? Do a spot of quick mental arithmetic at the start and quickly calculate how much time you have available to spend on each question. Add some extra time to your calculations for planning and checking too! You can practise your time management by answering questions from past papers.

7. Write neatly and legibly. If the examiner can't read your wildly illegible handwriting it's a fair bet that the majority of your information will get lost and this can cost marks.

8. Leave time at the end of the exam to proofread your answers. Correct any obvious errors. (It's a good idea to double space

your writing – leave a blank line between each written line
– so that you can go back and add corrections more easily
without leaving your answer in a mess!)

9. Plan your answers before you write. Use SPRE (see
page 59) to help you break down the question and construct
your answer.

10. Writing for academic purpose means writing in a formal,
serious, impersonal style. Omit any examples of slang or
conversational language. When writing in the exam, adhere
to all the rules of written grammar and spelling.

Don't start second-guessing your notes and your work. If you
allow doubt to creep in at the last minute it can affect the confidence
of your answers. Stay focused and have faith in your own abilities.
If you've revised thoroughly and have followed your timetable
plan efficiently and if you've minimised potential surprises by
planning mentally and by reviewing past papers, your anxiety
levels should be under control. If you still feel nervous, stick to
your routine.

QUICK TIP

Often exams come in blocks over a couple of weeks so stay in the 'exam
taking zone' until all of your exams are finished. When one's finished, focus
on the next exam and prepare thoroughly for it. Don't take your eye off the
ball until the final exam is completed.

After the exam

When the invigilator says 'Stop writing,' that's the end of it. No
amount of post-mortem discussions with friends in which you
analyse what you wrote and what you forgot will change the

answers you've submitted. It's best not to discuss it with anyone or, if you must, discuss what you did in general terms rather than in specifics. Remember, just because someone else wrote something you didn't, it doesn't mean their answer is better; everything depends on context and argument. Have faith in yourself, tick this one off and get ready for the next one.

Tips for top scores

■ Your exam timetable will tell you when the exams are. You can use this to prioritise when to start revision for specific topics.

■ Try working in short bursts rather than for hours at a time: this will help maintain your concentration levels.

■ Get a good night's sleep before the exam. Be rested and ready, physically and mentally.

■ Sit mock exams using past papers – you can do this with friends and compare answers at the end.

✓ Dos	✗ Don'ts
✓ Create a clear but realistic timetable.	✗ Leave revision until the last minute. Cramming for exams rarely works.
✓ Allocate time for different topics or areas on your course and distribute your study time as evenly as possible.	✗ Depend on your memory alone to get you through. Develop an understanding of the wider discussion and issues connected to aspects of your course.
✓ Use past exam papers to familiarise yourself with the exam paper layout and the kinds of questions usually asked.	✗ Study alone all the time. Join study groups and bounce ideas around with classmates.
✓ Work on your time management in exams by doing a dry practice run with past exam papers – using the set time limits to answer the correct number of questions.	✗ Stay up all night the day before the exam – get some rest and ensure you're mentally alert on the big day!
✓ Make sure you answer the set question! There's little worse than spending an hour writing an answer and then realising that you've missed the point.	
✓ Keep calm, stay organised and do your best, that's all anyone can ask!	

9 Drawing it all together

People commonly say that their university years are the best years of their life and they're right! University offers so many great opportunities socially and academically and you should take advantage of as many of these opportunities as you can.

However, while it's important to get the most out of your university social and sporting life it's equally important not to forget the real reason why you're at university in the first place: to study and obtain a degree.

You've already made an excellent first step in reading this book. It means you're serious about your student experience and you're interested in making sure your university years are fun **and** successful.

In the end, life at university, like life in general, comes down to **balance**. It can be difficult to make sure this juggling act doesn't spiral out of control, as it so easily can when the pressure's on, but you can maintain balance by focusing on ways to stay on track and sticking to your plans.

Achieving balance

Different people are successful for different reasons; just because one set of study habits suits one individual doesn't mean the same approach will work for you too. It's worth thinking about your previous learning experiences, at school or college, and evaluating what method of study fits best with your learning style.

This self-evaluation will help you develop your time management skills and help you structure a useful, productive and practical timetable for study and, later, for revision.

Maintaining balance

Maintaining balance means setting goals and reaching them within a set time frame. Review objectives regularly. Keep track of your progress and tick off objectives when you've achieved them: this will help you keep on top of what there is left to do.

Sticking to your plans means being well organised and good organisation boils down to the ability to think ahead and plan out a number of different things all at the same time. To do this it helps visualise objectives and outcomes and timetable accordingly depending on urgency and importance.

Making a timetable can be useful to help you prioritise your objectives.

- Have your lecture and class timetable, your assignment deadlines and exam dates clearly laid out.
- Add study group meetings and tutorials.

You will soon have a clearer picture of how your time should be divided over the coming term or semester. Once these fundamental commitments have been factored in, the next step is prioritising the remaining time into tasks and activities that will contribute to achieving your visualised outcomes. Pretty soon you will feel a sense of empowerment because, rather than letting circumstances swamp you, you are taking control!

Taking control

Taking control means taking responsibility. In the end, the balance of your success lies with you. The truth is that all students are in the same boat and achievement does not depend only on intelligence. Ultimately, the difference also comes down to control.

At school or college a lot of the responsibility for your studies was assumed by your teacher: if you didn't understand something you could just go to the teacher and they'd help you out. At university, tutors and lecturers expect you to be able to take much more care of yourself. In tutorials, for example, when tutors are available to help you, they much prefer you to come up with possible solutions to problems you'd like to discuss, rather than simply turning up with a problem and expecting a solution.

Maintaining your focus

You should certainly start as you mean to go on – but it's easy to let your initial planning and good intentions slip when you realise how much extracurricular fun there is to be had! Universities make entertainment a key consideration for their students. You are encouraged to get involved in social groups or sports teams and there's nothing wrong with enjoying your spare time. However, just remember to factor this leisure time into your timetable – that way, you won't lose sight of the balance between academic obligations and social commitments.

Don't rest on your laurels. Even if you are getting high grades and good marks, don't take your foot off the pedal. Positive feedback is great for morale and should boost your confidence in your own ability, but there's always room for improvement. Read feedback carefully and actively work on areas that need improving so that your next assignment is better. Aim for an upward curve of improvement and development.

A final word

It's easy to let the pressure get to you – and it gets to everyone at some point or another. The important thing is to try to plan out potential crises. Keeping an eye open for potential pitfalls or problematic areas can help you sidestep or avoid most of them. Reviewing objectives and staying on track can help you feel in control and this will help keep you calm and focused.

It's easy to say this (especially when exam dates or essay deadlines are looming), but enjoy your time at university. You're building your future, challenging yourself to achieve a worthwhile goal and you'll make lifelong friends along the way to boot!

It's important to keep reminding yourself that you are the master of your own destiny. With dedication and a good work ethic and hopefully with some of the ideas, tips and techniques covered in this book, you'll quickly realise that nothing is beyond your grasp!

Good luck!

Tips for top scores

■ Maintain a clear and regularly updated timetable that includes all your class, lecture and tutorial slots, assignment deadlines and exam dates as well as any extracurricular activities.

■ You will find that meeting assignment deadlines is easier if you have plenty of time to plan in advance. You will submit better work if you're able to work at a comfortable pace than you will if you work in a hurry because you failed to plan up front.

■ Keep focused. There's always room for improvement, so strive to submit work that's always better than your previous assignment. Try to keep grades moving on an upward trend.

✓ Dos	✗ Don'ts
✓ Make the most of the extracurricular activities offered by the university – get involved!	✗ Become isolated. Establish good lines of communication between yourself and the university, lecturers and tutors and your department. Gather all the right email addresses and telephone numbers.
✓ Maintain a tight timetable and keep study materials well organised so that they are of good use to you later on.	✗ Ignore feedback – useful advice from your tutor will help you see what areas of your work need improvement. Act on the advice and you'll notice your grades improving too!

Study skills Q & A

Why is it important to find out what kind of learner I am?

It's important because study experiences vary from individual to individual. Knowing who you are as a learner will affect the study habits you choose to adopt while also helping you get the most from sessions like seminars and lectures. See Chapter 1 for tips.

What if I'm the kind of person who finds it really difficult to stick to timetables and gets easily distracted?

Well, it's good to be honest with yourself. Admitting that you are the sort of student who can get distracted means you're taking a realistic outlook. You can help yourself by working out a timetable for study that realistically encompasses your limitations and sets out a programme that you're more likely to follow. Of course, you could help yourself even more by turning off Facebook or lending your Xbox to a friend for a fortnight so you won't be tempted! See Chapters 1 and 9 for more information.

How can I learn to work well under pressure?

By first spending time thinking about how to organise and plan your time and study habits. The better prepared you are and the more meticulous your organisation, the better you'll function in meeting deadlines. See the section on time management in Chapter 1 for some useful advice.

Is the critical thinking approach the only way?

No, but it is the approach expected in the majority of higher education institutions in the UK. Don't think of it as a doctrine that you're being forced to follow; think of it as the best, most logical, practical and ultimately most productive and insightful approach to comprehending and engaging with an academic discussion. It makes study easier by providing a systematic framework for tackling tough assignments. See Chapter 3 for more.

If I miss lectures or seminars for some reason, how can I recover that lost information?

Your department is likely to have a VLE, such as Blackboard. Often materials from lectures and seminars are posted there. Be sure you know where your departmental site is and how to access it. Another option is to email the lecturer directly asking for missed materials. One further option is to ask friends if you can photocopy handouts or even see their notes. See Chapter 7 on how to search for information independently.

What can I do if I can't listen, understand and write at the same time in lectures?

You can record lectures on your phone or on a Dictaphone. That way you can listen for detail later. Taking notes is important, but gaining overall comprehension is essential too. See Chapters 4 and 5 for more information on note taking and getting the most from lectures and seminars.

With so much information, how can I know what resources to use?

You'll be given a recommended reading list which will get you started. You'll find that you will use your reading list rather like links on web pages; reading one article or book chapter will lead you to similar or opposing sources. There are ways of evaluating sources too. See Chapter 7 for more details.

I always freeze up in exams: what can I do?

First, prepare well. The better prepared you are the more confident and relaxed you'll be. In fact once you feel prepared you might even find that you can't wait to get started, so that you can demonstrate what you know. Second, look at past exam papers. This will help you familiarise yourself with the layout and instructions as well as the type of questions you're likely to come across. Third, work out a study timetable and do your best to stick to it. The best way to reduce exam nerves is to be confident you'll have something to say. Finally, relax as much as possible. There are always resits (the opportunity to try again) and, while you should not rely on being able to resit a paper, it helps to know that if you do mess up in the exam it's not the end of the world. See Chapter 8 for more advice.

Glossary

Abstract
A brief summary of a research article, review or thesis; usually found at the beginning of an article or text.

Blackboard
A type of virtual learning environment (VLE) used by academic departments for storing or posting information relating to their courses.

Citation
Reference made to the original author(s) from whom ideas or information have been taken or used.

Critical thinking
An approach to academic study in which assumptions are questioned and evaluated.

Discursive
An argument or paper that discusses a topic and reaches a conclusion through reasoned argument.

Harvard (APA) system
A common referencing and bibliographical system used by most universities.

Literature review
A body of text that aims to review the critical points of current knowledge as well as theoretical and substantive knowledge of a topic or subject.

Past papers
Exam papers from previous years; can be used to practise for exams.

Plagiarism
The act of passing off someone else's work as your own without including appropriate citation.

Procrastination
To put something off until a later date with no good reason for doing so.

Proofread
To double check the accuracy and meaning of written work before submitting it.

Register
The tone and style of writing; a formal register is expected in academic communication at university level.

Seminar
A class or group in which ideas or topics related to a course are discussed and debated.

SMART
A system for planning goals or targets; stands for Specific, Measurable, Achievable, Realistic, Time-based.

SPRE
A system for deconstructing essay questions and formulating a written response; stands for Situation, Problem, Response, Evaluation.

Synthesis
The act of connecting information from a variety of sources into a coherent line of argument.

Thesis
A brief statement that summarises the writer's position in relation to a question or topic.

Tutorial
A short time slot in which students can meet their tutor to discuss problems or ask study-related questions.

Vancouver system
A numerical system of referencing, used mainly in medical disciplines.

Virtual learning environments (VLEs)
Online learning resources often managed by universities' libraries and departments.